Stinky Science

Why the Smelliest Smells Smell So Smelly

Written by **Edward Kay**

Illustrated by **Mike Shiell**

KIDS CAN PRESS

Get a Whiff of This!

You hold in your hands a veritable guide to the
gross, a manual of the malodorous, a syllabus of stenches.
Stinky Science reveals the secrets of smelliness,
whether it's scuzzy socks or stinky skunks.
A considerable amount of sweat has been expended
in researching this book. Hopefully it just smells like paper
and printers' ink — although if other people have read it
before you, there may also be what is sometimes
known as "grubby little fingers" odor.
So take a deep breath — through your nose, of course —
and prepare to become a scholar of stinks.

Contents

Why Some Things Stink — and How You Know They Do

If you've ever had the disgustingly unpleasant experience of getting a whiff of rotting garbage on a hot summer's day, you may have wondered: "Why do I have to smell bad things? Wouldn't life be sweeter if I didn't have to smell all those stinky stinks?"

Maybe — if we couldn't detect stinky things our life might smell sweeter, but it would probably be much shorter, too. We might even have become extinct long ago. Humans and other creatures have evolved a sense of smell to help us figure out which things are good for us and which things are dangerous.

You've probably noticed that when you have a bad cold and your nose is stuffed up, you can't smell things nearly as well. And your food probably doesn't taste as good either. That's because what we think of as the "flavor" of a particular food is really a combination of the way it tastes *and* smells, since our senses detect both at the same time. A number of more serious medical conditions can cause you to lose your sense of smell permanently, a condition called *anosmia*.

Losing your sense of smell can lead to feelings of depression, and it can definitely keep you from detecting things that are dangerous.

Where There's Smoke, There's Fire

If we smell a strong smell of smoke, such as when a building is burning down, it smells really, really bad. If you're like most people, smoke not only smells bad, it also makes you feel nervous.

It may seem strange that just the smell of something can have that effect on you. But there's a reason for it: your instincts tell you to go into a high-alert state when you smell smoke. When your *scent receptors* detect that smell, they send a signal to your brain. And even if you've never smelled a building on fire before, your instincts tell you that the smell is coming from something dangerous, and you need to get away from it as quickly as you can.

That's part of our *fight, flight or freeze* response, the same instinct that told our ancestors to be scared of a tiger if they saw one lurking in the forest. Even if they had never seen a tiger before, they didn't need to think about it. Their bodies would get a surge of *adrenaline*, and they would instinctively know to run, fight or hide.

Fee, Fie, Foe, Funky

Using those same instincts, our brains tell us that other dangerous things smell bad, too.

Rotting flesh smells disgusting to us. However, you may be surprised to know that the gross smell you inhale if you take a whiff of a rotting fish, for example, is not from the fish at all. It is from the bacteria living in the dead fish.

Warning: Microorganisms Live Here

The wretchedly horrible smells of rotting flesh are caused by *microorganisms* called *bacteria* and *fungi*. Microorganisms are living things that are so tiny, you cannot see them with your naked eye. They can be seen only through a microscope. Microorganisms produce these stinky stinks either by releasing chemicals from the rotting material that they decompose, or by making those stinky chemicals themselves.

Even though your eyes can't see microorganisms, your nose can smell them!

In the case of rotting fish, those bacteria convert trimethylamine oxide — a chemical that fish use to counteract the effects of salt water so they don't die of dehydration — into trimethylamine, which gives off the characteristic "fishy" odor. That's a good thing, because when microorganisms set up house in fish, meat or other food, they create toxins that can give us food poisoning.

You Can Rot, But You Can't Hide!

Some animals, such as vultures, have evolved so that they don't get sick from eating carrion. *Carrion* is a word for the rotting meat of dead animals that smell so bad, you probably wouldn't even want to get close enough to them to poke them with a stick.

Animals that eat carrion are called *scavengers*. To a vulture, a skunk that's been hit by a car and left rotting in the sun on a highway might smell as mouthwateringly yummy as chocolate cake with a side order of fries does to you.

However, a human body cannot digest rotting meat. If you eat it, you will get very, very sick. Maybe even die!

Then, you, too, would become very stinky … and very yummy-smelling to vultures! So if you eat rotten meat and die … well, don't say I didn't warn you.

You've Been Warned

But you won't eat rotten meat and die, will you? First of all, you've been warned.

And second, if you smell rotten meat, those scent detectors in your nose will send a signal to your brain that will tell you eating it would be a very bad idea!

There may actually have been some people throughout history whose brains thought the smell of rotting meat was yummy or who couldn't smell it at all. But those people probably died from eating that rotten meat before they could have children and pass along their genes to them. And that's why we have evolved so that many things that are bad for us smell bad to us, too!

Odorless Offenders

One important caveat (that's a fancy word for "warning")
is that not all bacteria that can make you sick or kill you
has a strong smell. *Salmonella* is a type of bacteria found
in the intestines of birds and mammals. Thousands of
people get sick from salmonella every year, and some
people even die.

But you can't tell if meat is contaminated with
salmonella just by smelling it. You need to test it in a
lab. That may be why salmonella poisoning is the most
common form of food poisoning — because we humans
have not evolved any means of smelling it.

Fortunately, we *have* evolved a clever brain that has
helped us figure out the conditions that allow salmonella
to contaminate our food, and we've learned how to avoid
them. For example, you should make sure that your eggs
and poultry are well cooked and that food is properly
refrigerated. Wash your hands after touching animals,
especially reptiles like turtles, snakes and lizards. And you
should especially avoid licking live rattlesnakes, or you'll
have a whole new set of problems.

How You Smelt What You Got Dealt

Your sense of smell is a highly effective detection instrument. In your body, there are more genes devoted to smell than to any of your other senses. As a result, you are able to identify 10 000 unique smells — some of them nice and some of them as horrible as the ones you're about to discover.

The reason you are so easily able to smell the difference between petunias and poop is that way up inside your nose, at the back and just below your brain, is an area called the *olfactory epithelium*. On it, you have about six million scent receptors.

We're not sure who counted them all, because even if you could look up your own nose or somebody else's with a magnifying glass, you wouldn't be able to see them. They are so tiny that they're only visible when magnified thousands of times through an electron microscope.

Your Nose Knows

Six million is a lot of scent receptors. If every single person living in Denmark were a scent receptor, that's how many you'd have in your nose.

But you would need to have an extremely large nose to fit all those people in there.

And if all those people were scent receptors, they'd gross each other out, because your actual scent receptors are covered with *mucus*, which is another word for snot.

Detecting the Undelectable

So how do those scent receptors actually detect something nasty and tell us that it's a bad smell? Scents reach your receptors through your nostrils and through a second passage, a channel that connects the roof of the throat to the nose.

Here's a perfectly stinky example of how it works. Poop smells bad because the dead and live bacteria in it make chemicals, including hydrogen sulfide gas, that combine to make a really foul odor. If you have ever walked into a bathroom where someone has forgotten to flush the toilet after they have taken a poop, you will know that the air in it does not smell anything like evergreen tree–scented air freshener (unless that person tried to wipe their bum with pine needles, which is almost as bad an idea as eating rotten meat).

Poop is made up of dead and live bacteria, undigested food, dead blood cells and mucus.

Malodorous Molecules

So here's the really gross part. The reason that you can smell poop nearby is because tiny bits of that poop are actually floating through the air and going up your nose!

A *molecule* is the smallest physical unit of an element or compound. In the case of an element, the molecule is made up of two or more of the same type of atoms, while in a compound, the molecule consists of two or more different types of atoms. The good news is that there is no such thing as a "poop molecule."

However, there are molecules of other chemicals that, when we smell them all at the same time, make the odor we recognize as poop. One of the molecules that makes up that icky smell is mercaptan, also known as methanethiol.

Mercaptan molecules are also found in bad breath and many of the other unpleasant smells you will encounter in this book. A molecule of mercaptan is made up of atoms of carbon, hydrogen and sulfur, and it looks like this:

mercaptan

Indole is another type of chemical found in poop. Its molecules look like this:

indole

There are a number of other chemicals that, when combined with the molecules above, our brains recognize as the smell of poop.

What Smell Is Your Shape?

But here's something really amazing. Those molecules don't actually have any smell of their own. Yes, you read that right. They don't actually have any smell. None at all. Nada.

When you breathe in through your nose, smells are processed by your *olfactory bulb*, which is a part of your brain located right behind your nose. The olfactory bulb is directly connected to two parts of your brain that process emotions and memory: the *amygdala* and *hippocampus*.

The molecules you inhale stimulate a combination of scent receptors, creating a unique representation in the brain. The sensors in your olfactory epithelium recognize the shape of those molecules and send a signal to your brain, which assigns a smell to each shape so it can recognize them. It's sort of like the way we give each other names so it's easier for us to explain who we are talking about. As in "Did you happen to catch a whiff of the bathroom? I think Ziggy forgot to flush the toilet again."

Thanks for Flushing

Here's something else that's amazing. Girls have a better sense of smell than boys. That's because girls have more cells in their olfactory bulb than boys. So if someone forgets to flush that toilet, it probably smells even grosser to a girl than to a boy.

But don't worry. No matter whether you're a boy or a girl, smelling poop in the tiny, tiny amounts that you inhale in a bathroom won't hurt you. Even so, it's always polite to flush the toilet after you're done. Because nobody likes their scent receptors to have to tell their brain that they have just inhaled bits of someone else's poop!

The Unforgettable Funk: Smell and Memory

A French writer named Marcel Proust is famous for having noticed how our sense of smell can make us suddenly remember things. Proust wrote a novel called *In Search of Lost Time*. In it, the narrator smells a type of small sponge cake called a madeleine, which smells much nicer than most of the odors described in this book.

The character in Proust's book is surprised to find that the scent of the madeleine causes him to suddenly remember a bunch of happy times — although the truth is that people were aware of the relationship between our memories and our sense of smell long before the French author became a world-renowned madeleine-sniffer.

Stanks for the Memory

Your sense of smell is so strongly connected to your memory that it can actually be used to help you remember things that you might otherwise forget.

In China, there is a centuries-old custom of passing around a pot of spices while telling a story so that the people who are hearing the story will remember it in the future when they smell the same scent. Unlike unflushed toilets, spices smell good to most people. That's why we put them in our food.

Not-So-Sweet Memories

But bad smells can make you remember things just as easily as good smells.

Suppose that the people who passed around a pot of spices took turns sniffing something gross instead — like rotten eggs and dung, for example. If they were unfortunate enough to smell those scents again, they would remember the story just as well as if they had heard it while sniffing spices. Eww.

And if you smelled a very bad smell while you were reading this book … and then were fortunate enough not to smell that smell again for many, many years — until you were as old as your grandparents — your brain would still remember that smell.

In fact, that awful aroma would make such an impression on your brain that if you were to get a whiff of it years later, two things would happen. First, you would immediately remember having once inhaled that smell. Second, you might recall other memories you thought you had forgotten.

For example, you might suddenly remember what else was happening the first time you smelled that scent and who else was with you — and if their eyes were bugging out and they were throwing up in their mouth just a little! It might also make you remember whether it was cold or warm, sunny or rainy, and even if you were feeling happy or sad at the time. That's how strongly our sense of smell is connected to our memory.

I've Got a Bad Feeling About This

Your other senses — sight, sound, touch and taste — can *trigger* involuntary memories, too. But your sense of smell is unique in that it is more closely linked to your emotions than your other senses. Smells can actually change your mood by triggering good or bad memories.

Even a good smell can make you feel bad if your memory connects it with something unpleasant. Imagine that while riding your bike as fast as you can go, you sniff one of Proust's madeleines. The sweet smells of vanilla, sugar and lemon baked into that delicious little sponge cake might distract you so much that you lose control of your bike, careen off the road and crash into a zombie- and leech-infested swamp where the locals chase you to eat your brain and suck you dry.

Assuming that you survive, if you smell a madeleine again, you probably will experience unpleasant emotions such as fear, even though the madeleine smells good. Unfortunately, you'll forever associate that enticing aroma with your misadventures in the swamp.

Stinky Sweet

Strange as it might sound, the opposite is true, too. Even smells that we usually think of as stinky can trigger happy memories and emotions if people first smelled them when they were doing something they enjoyed.

Odoriferous and Awesome Outer Space

For example, astronauts say that outer space has a distinctive smell. But nobody can stick their head out into space and sniff it. That's because space is a vacuum. If someone stuck their head out of a spaceship without wearing a space suit and helmet, their head would explode!

So how do we know what space smells like? We know because astronauts say that the space suits they wear during space walks have a particular smell on the outside after they come back from being worn in space.

The distinctive smell is created by chemicals called *polycyclic aromatic hydrocarbons*. Those chemicals are found here on Earth, too. You can smell them in *fossil fuels* such as diesel and coal, especially when they make a lot of smoke. You can also smell them in cigarette smoke

and in food that gets barbecued so long that it turns into a bunch of blackened cinders. That's not an odor that most people like.

But astronauts love their work. They train for years for a chance to go out into space. And only a handful of the astronauts who blast off into orbit ever get to actually walk in space. So when they finally get to float around outside their spaceship, gazing at the spectacular sight of the universe around them and planet Earth below, it's a thrilling experience.

So, even though their space suit might smell like a combination of school bus exhaust and incinerated hamburger, astronauts associate that odor with a dream come true. It's a stinky smell, but it helps them remember all the positive emotions associated with an amazing experience.

Toot Sweet

French inventor Christian Poincheval invented a pill that he claims will make your farts smell like chocolate, so that they won't stink up your home or classroom.

So if everyone started tooting out chocolate-scented farts, does that mean that people would start to have happy memories when they smelled farts? Or would it just make people suddenly have bad memories whenever they smelled chocolate? Only time will tell.

How Do Smells Trigger Memories and Emotions?

Scientists believe that smells trigger memories and emotions because of the anatomy of our brains.

Remember the olfactory bulb and how it's connected to the amygdala and the hippocampus, the two parts of your brain that process emotion and memory? That means the "smell" information collected by your olfactory bulb doesn't have to travel far to get to the parts of your brain associated with emotion and memory. By contrast, information gathered by your senses of sight, sound and touch must travel much farther, through many more connections — called synapses — before they reach the amygdala and hippocampus.

Scientists believe that you remember smells more easily because signals related to smell have a much more direct path to the part of your brain that processes memory.

Stinkiest Stinks: Icky Animals and Vile Vegetation

Animals produce bad smells for a number of reasons. Some use them as a defense against *predators*, others use them to mark their territory, and still others use them to attract mates — hey, whatever works!

Some plants send out sweet scent signals to attract insects. Other plants stink.

Pee-ew, a Polecat

If you've upset a skunk, you'll know that it can create a very unpleasant smell. Chemicals known as *thiols* are responsible for the stinkiest part of a skunk's spray. They are found in garlic and onions, too.

But the honor of being the world's stinkiest animal goes to the polecat.

Despite its name, the polecat is not a cat but a member of the weasel family. It marks its territory with — get this — its own poop. If threatened, the polecat will defend itself by shooting out an "anal spray" (in other words, a spray that it shoots out of its bum).

The polecat's spray also contains thiols, but it's seven times more powerful than a skunk's spray. The polecat's spray is so stinky that it can be smelled up to a mile away! It smells like a mixture of burned rubber, garlic, rotten eggs and a dirty gym locker.

The anal spray can temporarily blind an attacker and irritate its mucus glands (mostly in the nose), allowing the polecat to escape. The old saying goes that there's "safety in numbers," but clearly, there's safety in stink, too!

Beware the Bombardier Beetle

The polecat's defense is a breath of fresh air compared to that of an insect known as the bombardier beetle. When threatened, the bombardier beetle shoots out hydroquinone and hydrogen peroxide, which smell horrible when combined. They interact to create a high-pressure vapor jet almost as hot as boiling water that can actually kill an attacker.

Don't Scare the Green Wood Hoopoe

If you encounter the green wood hoopoe bird, be careful you don't frighten it, because the green wood hoopoe is one of the stinkiest animals in the world.

And if the green wood hoopoe thinks you are a predator, it will turn its bum toward you and spray you with a very stinky combination of chemicals, including dimethyl sulfide, which is what gives rotten eggs their putrid smell.

A baby green wood hoopoe can't create the same spray that its parents do, but it still has a trick up its sleeve (well, actually, up its bum). If frightened, it will spray you with liquid poop. Well, even hoopoes have to start somewhere.

Filthy As a Sloth

Sloths, on the other hand, smell bad just because of their slothful habits. They move slowly and don't do much of anything — including grooming.

As a result, sloths have *algae* and fungi growing on them. And insects. One study found that a single sloth had 980 beetles living in its fur. They share that space with up to 120 moths at a time. The moths eat secretions from the sloth's skin and feed on the algae that grow on it.

To round out the sloth's personal zoo, there are three kinds of mites that make their home not-so-sweet home in the sloth's bum!

Why Eat Durian Fruit?

It might not surprise you to learn that plants can attract flies by being stinky.

However, you might be surprised to learn that some stinky plants attract people, too, in particular, a stinky plant known as a durian fruit.

Durian is an Asian fruit whose fifty separate compounds combine to produce a scent that food writer Richard Sterling described as similar to "turpentine and onions, garnished with a gym sock."

So why would anybody want to eat durian fruit? One answer may be that they taste much different than they smell. One European explorer, when trying it for the first time, described the flavor as similar to custard and almonds. Some researchers point to genetic differences in the people doing the smelling and tasting. Some people don't smell the compounds that other people find so gross, so they get to enjoy the custard flavor without thinking about sloth bums.

The Odoriferous Case of the Corpse Plant

Take the case of the corpse plant, the biggest flower in the world. It can grow up to 3 m (9.8 ft.) high and lives in the jungles of Indonesia.

If you guessed that the corpse plant got its name because it smells as though a big disgusting hairy animal with mites living in its bum crawled into it, then died and became even stinkier by rotting … you'd be right.

Now, given that some flowers, such as roses and jasmine, smell sweet and pleasing to us, you may wonder why the corpse plant chose the opposite tactic. The answer is that just like other plants, the corpse plant needs to attract insects to carry its pollen to other plants of its species so it can reproduce.

Most flowers attract insects by smelling good, to advertise the fact that they have sweet nectar inside. But in the jungles where the corpse plant lives, there are millions of wonderful-smelling plants that compete with each other to attract pollinating insects.

If a corpse plant smelled sweet, too, it would have lots of competition from other plants to attract those insects. So the corpse plants have adapted by taking a different approach. They smell really, really bad in order to attract the sorts of insects that prefer rotting meat and dung over sweet nectar. Flies and beetles are attracted to the corpse plant because its hideously horrible odor tricks them into thinking that they are smelling rotting flesh, which they like to both eat and lay their eggs in — yuck!

The Structure of Stinks

Of course, you couldn't have stinky plants or stinky bugs or stinky animals with bugs living in their stinky bums if you didn't have the building blocks of stink: chemicals.

All those stinks are made by combinations of chemicals that we instinctively dislike, such as mercaptans and thiols, and the ones made by rotting corpses, including carboxylic acids, aromatics, sulfurs, alcohols, nitro compounds, as well as aldehydes and ketones. Some stinky chemicals, such as formaldehyde, are dangerous for you to even smell, so stay away from them!

Putrid Pairs

Because everything in our world is made up of combinations of atoms and molecules, including stinky things, sometimes those stinky compounds turn up in things that you might not realize have something chemically in common. For example … cheese.

Limburger, one of the stinkiest cheeses on the planet, smells like dirty feet because it contains *Brevibacterium linens*, the same microbe that is responsible for making dirty feet smell stinky.

Stinky Foot Cheese?

Yes, as disgusting as it sounds, stinky feet and certain cheeses smell the same because something in them *is* the same: the microorganism responsible for the stinky feet smell is also used to ferment milk in the notoriously stinky Limburger cheese.

You might wonder why people who find the odor of dirty feet unpleasant aren't offended by cheese that smells almost the same and has a very similar microbe living in it. Nobody really knows. (Of course, there are people who don't like the smell of stinky feet who probably don't like the smell of stinky cheese either.)

Shark Meat or Wet Diaper?

But cheese isn't the only food that has something in common with something you wouldn't want to smell. Hákarl is an Icelandic dish made from fermented Greenland shark. Flesh of the Greenland shark is poisonous when it is fresh, but allowing the meat to decay removes the toxins, making it edible — if extremely stinky!

The strong smell of hákarl is the result of ammonia, a compound made of hydrogen and nitrogen atoms. Ammonia smells extremely unpleasant to humans. Besides being found in hákarl, it is also a very smellable component of many cleaning products, such as glass cleaner, and if you have a baby sister or baby brother who still wears diapers, you might be able to catch a whiff of it wherever wet diapers are discarded.

Kissing Cousins

Getting back to the subject of similar stinks, *halitosis* (bad breath) and rotting cabbage also smell similar, because you could say that, chemically speaking, they are kissing cousins. Although very few people will be interested in kissing you if you smell like rotten cabbage or have bad breath.

Both contain methyl mercaptan, a substance that can often be found wherever things get stinky.

Swamp Bum

Two other unpleasant odors that smell similar because they share similar chemistry are farts and swamps full of rotting vegetation. Among other things, they both contain a stinky chemical called hydrogen sulfide. If you find it unpleasant to think of smelling a fart or a swamp full of rotting plants (and possibly rotting zombies), tell yourself instead that you're smelling rotten eggs, which also contain hydrogen sulfide.

Stink or Swim

Some of the most expensive perfumes in the world contain a rare substance called ambergris. The reason it's so rare is that it only comes from certain kinds of sperm whales, specifically from their intestines, when they poop it out — which is probably why people who have smelled ambergris say its odor is like manure.

Why would you want to smell like manure? Apparently, after twenty or thirty years of floating around in the ocean, ambergris acquires a sweet smell, too. The three main chemical components of ambergris are triterpene alcohol ambrein, epicoprostanol and coprostanone.

Another component of some perfumes is civet oil, taken from the anal glands of the civet, a small, catlike mammal. This secretion is said to smell absolutely horrible in its natural state. But apparently, when diluted and allowed to age, it acquires a sweetness that some people find pleasant.

Hate Your Perfume, Darling

Not everyone finds perfume pleasant. In fact, some people find it so unpleasant that many workplaces and other public spaces are now "scent-free," meaning that you are asked not to wear perfume or aftershave. Not covering yourself with sperm whale *excreta* or civet anal gland secretions is probably a good idea, too.

So why do some people find some smells pleasant while others find them horrible? Researchers think that some people have a more finely tuned sense of smell, so they can detect unpleasant odors that other people don't notice, or they smell them more strongly. Another theory is that while most people don't notice a particular odor after they've been smelling it for a few minutes, other people's brains are wired so that the smell doesn't "wear off." Stinky perfume smells just as strong to them an hour later as it did the first moment it wafted its way up their nostrils.

One reason people created artificial scents is that throughout most of our history, we humans probably smelled worse than the smells that we now find offensive.

For various reasons, certain human cultures were unable or unwilling to bathe and wash regularly, which would have been unfortunate for anyone close enough to get a whiff. Because although our perspiration doesn't smell bad, microbes that like to eat certain compounds in our sweat excrete substances that definitely *do* stink — like trans-3-methyl-2-hexenoic acid, which you might be more familiar with as

"b.o." (body odor). In earlier times, people from the ancient Egyptians to the Victorians concocted all manner of ways to cover up their stink, such as colognes. Incense was burned inside churches and other places where people gathered together, creating a collective pong that must have been truly wretched.

Now that we are generally less stinky than our ancestors, it's no longer necessary to fill public spaces with artificial scents. But that doesn't mean we don't do it anymore. In fact, thanks to modern technology, restaurants and even vending machines can use the artificial smells of popcorn, cinnamon buns, waffle cones, sugar cookies, coffee, chocolate and even grilled hamburgers to tempt your appetite — through your nose!

Super Sniffers

Which creatures have the best senses of smell? Drop dead and you'll find out very quickly.

Scent Detectives

Remember that vulture you read about earlier? To help them find yummy dead things that are far away, vultures have hundreds of millions of scent receptors in their noses. That's many, many times more scent detectors than you have in your nose.

Superdogs

Dogs also have many, many more scent detectors in their noses than we do. Because of that, dogs are used by hunters to detect prey. They are also used to find lost children, as well as sniff out bombs and drugs. Other dogs are specially trained to smell cadavers. These dogs are used by police forces to find victims of accidents and murders. Some dogs' noses are so sensitive that they can use their sense of smell to locate buried fragments of bodies just a few inches long. Other cadaver dogs have the incredible ability to sniff out bodies that are under water.

Doggy Delicacies

Speaking of stinky, rotten dead things, you might wonder why, if dogs have such a powerful sense of smell, they eat things with such vile aromas. The answer is that to dogs, those things don't smell vile at all. To a dog, the chemicals given off by rotting meat smell great! That's because, like vultures, dogs have digestive systems that have adapted to eating dead things that would make us sick.

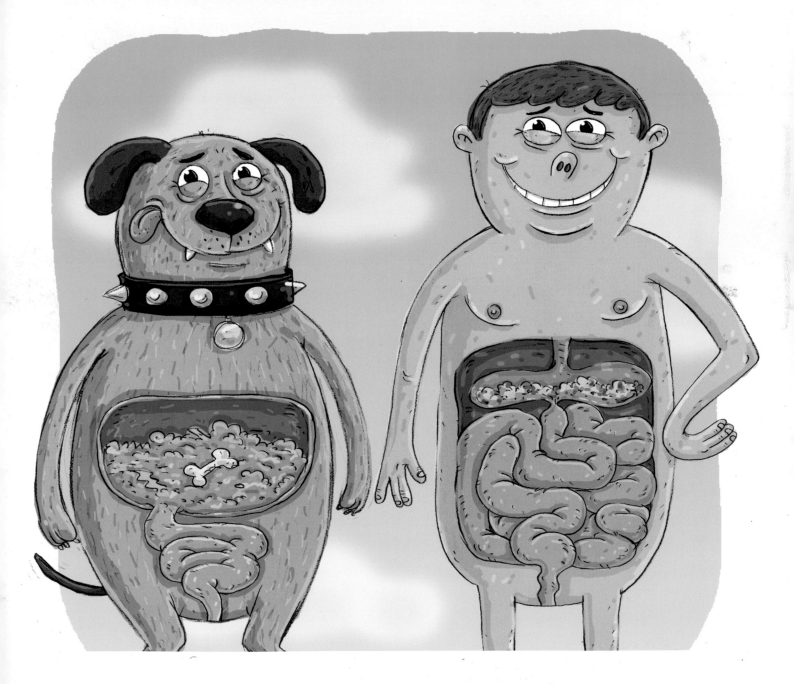

Smells Like Dinner

Carrion — the decaying flesh of dead animals — is an important food source for many wild animals, including eagles, Komodo dragons and man's best friend's cousins, the wolf and the coyote. They are all quite happy not to have to hunt and kill for their dinner if their dinner is considerate enough to save them all that trouble by dying first.

No Swimming with the Sharks

On the other hand, you don't even need to be dead for a shark to quickly sniff you out. Sharks can detect a single drop of blood in the water from 3.2 km (2 mi.) away. So if you have a cut on your finger or toe, avoid swimming with sharks. Actually, even if you don't have a cut on your finger or toe, swimming with sharks is not a great idea.

Two-thirds of a shark's brain is devoted to its sense of smell. Sharks also have very good hearing!

Something Fishy

The albatross, a bird that looks something like a huge seagull, uses its keen sense of smell to monitor many miles of ocean at a time and can detect schools of fish that are far out of sight.

Smelling in Stereo

The Eastern American mole lives underground in the dark and is virtually blind, so it has developed the handy ability to smell in stereo. In the same way that we can use our stereo hearing to tell whether something is to our left or right, the mole uses its stereo sense of smell to help it find its favorite food, the earthworm.

Scent Smarts

Of course, smell isn't always all about finding food. Sometimes the olfactory sense is used to avoid becoming food. Besides being able to locate tiny slivers of food from 50 m (165 ft.) away, smell distant water and distant mates, African elephants can actually smell the difference between two African ethnic groups of people, the Maasai and the Kamba. The elephant has a very good reason for having developed that ability. Young Maasai warriors prove their bravery by spearing elephants, while the Kamba are an agricultural people who pose no threat to the elephants.

Moth Mating

Many other animals also use their sense of smell to find a suitable mate. Using their antennae as their sense of "smell," tiny male silkworm moths can detect a female more than a half a mile away! That's like humans being able to smell a potential mate in a different city!

Smell Ya Later!

By now, you've learned a lot about why some things stink. And hopefully you appreciate that wonderful sense that's right at the tip of your nose. So like the old expression says, "Remember to stop and smell the roses." You just might want to avoid the corpse plants, poop and durian fruit!

Glossary

adrenaline: a hormone produced by the adrenal glands in your body. Adrenaline speeds up heart rates and breathing, and prepares muscles for action by making blood in the body circulate faster.

algae: a nonflowering plant group that includes seaweeds and many single-celled forms

amygdala: group of nuclei (more than one nucleus — a nucleus is the center of an atom) located in the temporal lobes of the brain. It performs a primary role in memory processing, decision-making and emotional reactions.

anosmia: the medical term for loss of the sense of smell

bacteria: tiny, living single-cell microorganisms that are neither plants nor animals

carrion: the decaying flesh of dead animals

excreta: waste material produced and discharged by a living being, for example, poop

fight, flight or freeze: your instinctive reaction when confronted with a perceived threat to either fight it, run away from it or freeze in the hope that it either won't notice you or will get bored with you and leave

fossil fuels: natural fuels such as coal or gas, formed millions of years ago from the remains of living organisms

fungi: a group of unicellular, multicellular or syncytial (having many nuclei but no cells) spore-producing organisms feeding on organic matter, including molds, yeast, mushrooms and toadstools

halitosis: scientific name for bad breath

hippocampus: the part of the brain thought to be the center of emotion, memory and the autonomic nervous system. (The autonomic nervous system controls certain processes in your body, such as how fast you breathe, automatically, without you trying.)

microorganism: a tiny, microscopic organism, especially a bacterium, virus or fungus. (Organisms are living beings, including animals, plants and single-celled life forms.)

molecule: a group of atoms bonded together, representing the smallest basic unit of a chemical compound that can take part in a chemical reaction

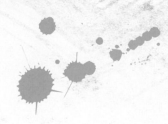

mucus: a thick liquid produced inside the nose and other parts of the body, sometimes known as snot

olfactory bulb: a structure located in the front part of the brain of humans and other vertebrates (animals with backbones) that receives neural input about odors detected by cells in the nasal cavity

olfactory epithelium: specialized tissue inside the nasal cavity above and behind the nostrils that is part of your odor-detection system

polycyclic aromatic hydrocarbons: organic compounds containing hydrogen and carbon

predator: an animal that obtains its food mainly by killing and eating other animals

salmonella: bacterium that causes food poisoning

scavenger: an animal that feeds on carrion, dead plant material or waste

scent receptors: cells that trigger nerve impulses that send information about odors to the brain

thiols: a particularly stinky category of chemical compounds that include rotten egg and skunk smells

trigger: to stimulate a reaction or series of reactions

Index

For my children, Alex and Mika, who share my fascination
with nature and science, and who smell much nicer than any
of the horrible substances described in this book — E.K.

To my wife, Mary, who has always believed in me even when
I doubted myself. She also smells way better than me. — M.S.

Text © 2019 Edward Kay
Illustrations © 2019 Mike Shiell

Kids Can Press gratefully acknowledges the financial support of the Government of
Ontario, through the Ontario Media Development Corporation; the Ontario Arts
Council; the Canada Council for the Arts; and the Government of Canada for our
publishing activity.

Published in Canada and the U.S. by Kids Can Press Ltd.
25 Dockside Drive, Toronto, ON M5A 0B5

Kids Can Press is a Corus Entertainment Inc. company

www.kidscanpress.com

The artwork in this book was rendered in pencil and completed in Photoshop.
The text is set in Bulmer.

Edited by Kathy Fraser
Designed by Julia Naimska

Printed and bound in Shenzhen, China, in 10/2018 by C & C Offset

CM 19 0 9 8 7 6 5 4 3 2 1

Library and Archives Canada Cataloguing in Publication

Kay, Edward, author
    Stinky science : why the smelliest smells smell so smelly / Edward Kay ;
illustrated by Mike Shiell.

Includes index.

ISBN 978-1-77138-382-0 (hardcover)

    1. Smell — Juvenile literature. 2. Nose — Juvenile literature. 3. Odors — Juvenile
literature. 4. Smell — Juvenile humor. 5. Nose — Juvenile humor. 6. Odors —
Juvenile humor. 7. Canadian wit and humor (English) — Juvenile literature.
8. Wit and humor, Juvenile.

I. Shiell, Mike, illustrator II. Title.

QP458.K39 2019   j612.8'6   C2018-902013-X